Women Of Calvary

A Play For Lent

Marguerite D. Brown

CSS Publishing Company, Inc., Lima, Ohio

WOMEN OF CALVARY

Copyright © 2006 by
CSS Publishing Company, Inc.
Lima, Ohio

The original purchaser may photocopy material in this publication for use as it was intended (worship material for worship use; educational material for classroom use; dramatic material for staging or production). No additional permission is required from the publisher for such copying by the original purchaser only. Inquiries should be addressed to: Permissions, CSS Publishing Company, Inc., 517 South Main Street, Lima, Ohio 45804.

Scripture quotations are from the New Revised Standard Version of the Bible, copyright 1989 by the Division of Christian Education of the National Council of the Churches of Christ in the USA. Used by permission.

Published previously in 1982; ISBN 0-89536-526-X

For more information about CSS Publishing Company resources, visit our website at www.csspub.com or email us at custserv@csspub.com or call (800) 241-4056.

Cover design by Barbara Spencer
ISBN 0-7880-2396-9   PRINTED IN U.S.A.

*This book is dedicated
to the memory of the
author, Marguerite D. Brown*

Table Of Contents

Director's Notes	7
Scene 1 The Upper Room	11
Scene 2 In The Courtyard	19
Scene 3 The Way To Golgotha	27
Scene 4 On The Way To The Tomb	33
Scene 5 The Waiting Place	39

Director's Notes

Characters
  Mary Magdalene
  Mary, mother of James and Joseph
  Salome, mother of James and John
  Mary, mother of Mark
  Claudia, wife of Pilate
  Julia, Claudia's maid
  Mary, mother of Jesus
  Mary, sister of Martha
  Martha
  Mark
  John
  Pilate
  Lazarus

Props
  Scene 1 — wine carafe or pitcher with four small cups on tray
  Scene 2 — Roman helmet on bench
  Scene 3 — no props
  Scene 4 — basket with vials and bottles, rolls of linens or sheets, and basket filled with jars and dried herbs
  Scene 5 — wooden trays and bowls placed on various benches

Costumes
The women's dresses should be simple one-piece robes. The headdresses are simple cloths, about one and one-half yards long. The colors should vary from dark blue or green to shades of rust and brown. Mary Magdalene wears a royal blue robe. The women in Scene 4 dress in black. Claudia wears a white robe with a jeweled belt and a pale blue chiffon scarf fastened to the shoulder and also a jeweled headband. Julia, Claudia's maid, wears a simple tunic with sash and a ribbon around her hair. Mark wears a simple

tunic with a short robe. John and Lazarus wear tunics with long robes and turbans. Pilate wears a tunic with pleats, reaching to the calf of the leg, a short leather breastplate, and a cape fastened at one shoulder. All wear sandals. Pilate has lacings up his legs.

Since there is no actual stage setting, more emphasis is placed on the costumes.

Setting

This play can be staged in front of the altar. Players enter from the sides of the altar. Benches or stools should be placed in front as needed. In Scene 3, Claudia tells about her dreams from the lectern, and in Scene 4, Mary Magdalene also gives her opening address from the lectern.

Time

Each scene takes approximately fifteen to twenty minutes.

Synopsis

Women Of Calvary can be presented as one play or as five short scenes for use during Lent. No setting is required and costuming is simple. *Women Of Calvary* can be presented in the chancel.

Scene 1: The Upper Room — After serving the Passover meal, Mary Magdalene; Mary, the mother of James and Joseph; Salome, the mother of James and John; and Mary, the mother of Mark, sit on the roof discussing the meal and what happened. Mark arrives to tell of the capture of Jesus.

Scene 2: In The Courtyard — Claudia, the wife of Pilate, is agitated by the news of Jesus' arrest. She sends her maid, Julia, for news. Claudia tells of her dreams and she confronts Pilate by stating that he is condemning an innocent man to death, for which he will never be forgiven.

Scene 3: The Way To Golgotha — Salome is comforting Mary, the mother of Jesus; they have heard the news of Jesus being taken before Pilate. Mary, the mother of James, and Mary, the mother of Mark, arrive with the latest news, and John comes to tell her that Jesus has been condemned and is on the way to Golgotha.

Scene 4: On The Way To The Tomb — Mary Magdalene tells of her early days before she met Jesus, how he healed her, how she became a follower, and then she tells of events up to his death on the cross. She is waiting for Salome and Mary, the mother of James, who will accompany her to the tomb.

Scene 5: The Waiting Place — Mary and Martha are preparing the evening meal and discussing the previous visit of Jesus. They discuss Lazarus and his return from death because of Jesus. Lazarus arrives to tell them what has happened in Jerusalem, ending with the taking of the body to the tomb. In the midst of their sorrow, Martha remembers what Jesus told her: "I am the resurrection and the life. Those who believe in me, even though they will die, will live" (John 11:25-26). The play ends on the affirmation of Martha.

Scene 1

The Upper Room

Characters
 Mary Magdalene
 Mary, mother of James and Joseph
 Salome, mother of James and John
 Mary, mother of Mark
 Mark

Setting
 The roof of the house where the Last Supper was held

(The four women enter, with Mary, mother of Mark, leading and carrying a tray with four small glasses and a carafe of wine. She passes the glasses to them as they take their places around the roof. Mary Magdalene goes to the edge of the roof and looks down at the valley.)

Mary Magdalene: It's quiet tonight, and so peaceful. Look at the moon. It is full.

Mary, mother of Mark: That is supposed to be a good omen for the Passover. It was a good Passover. The men seemed to enjoy it, and I am sure the Master did.

Salome: If you remember, the Master made all the special arrangements for this meal.

Mary, mother of Mark: That is true. Everything went well. But somehow it seemed different this year. Perhaps it was because it is the first time we have celebrated the Passover together, at least at this house.

Mary, mother of James: The men have grown so close together. They are truly followers of the Master. I remember when my sons first came to me and said they were leaving. I couldn't believe it — to give up all their livelihoods to follow a man.

Salome: I know. I felt the same way. Peter's wife was quite indignant. After all, he has a large family. But somehow they managed to survive, and the Master did heal her mother.

Mary, mother of James: I am glad they have permitted us to follow them. At least I can see my sons and know what they are doing and where they are.

Mary, mother of Mark: That is true, but really they need us. Who would prepare the meals, do the cooking, and do the washing?

Mary Magdalene: Time goes by so quickly. Has it been only a few months since we first met? And now look how our lives are entwined.

Mary, mother of James: It was only a few days ago when the Master rode into the city, and they welcomed him with palms and triumphant song. It was such a joyful occasion. I believed a new day was dawning. The people crowded around the Master and tried to touch him.

Salome: They wanted miracles again. He is always so patient with them. It seemed as if all of God's promises were coming true. The Messiah was really here and would take his throne.

Mary, mother of Mark: *(gets up, passes the wine around, talking as she does so)* I wonder what he will do when he is king. Will he take over Herod's palace? I, for one, wouldn't want it. They say it is drafty and the rooms are so large they echo.

Salome: You can always use rugs to help for that, but I don't think he will use that palace. Perhaps another one, near the temple or perhaps even on a hill. That would truly be a site for a palace with a view of everything he owns.

Mary, mother of James: But Peter says that isn't the kind of mansion he talks about. In fact, he never mentions a palace, but surely he will need one when he comes into his kingdom.

Mary Magdalene: It is so very quiet down there. *(goes to the edge and looks down)* You can almost see the garden from here. It is such a beautiful place. No wonder the Master likes to go there. *(returns to her place)*

Salome: There was one thing tonight. I thought it was terrible for the Master to wash the feet of all those men — and they *let* him. *They* should have been washing his feet. After all, he is the Master.

Mary Magdalene: I heard him say something about a master not being greater than the servant and that he had given them an example.

Mary, mother of Mark: Of course, we could only get snatches of the conversation when we brought in the foods, but sometimes the men seemed uneasy.

Mary, mother of James: Even the Master looked sad at times. Once, when I was bringing in the wine, I saw tears in his eyes.

Salome: I heard him say something about leaving them, but that where he was going, they could not come. But he said not to worry, he was preparing a place for them. I wonder where he will go. Perhaps to start his kingdom. But surely the Master would need his followers with him.

Mary Magdalene: I hope he is not leaving us. I want to spend all my days following him and serving him. But I can't help feeling uneasy tonight. Perhaps it is because there are so many people here in Jerusalem for the Passover.

Salome: They say they killed over 10,000 lambs at the temple. That should make old Ananias happy. He is always wanting to make a profit for the temple.

Mary, mother of James: They were certainly getting more shekels this year for the unblemished lambs.

Mary Magdalene: When I serve the Passover, I always think of our forefathers and how the Lord brought them safely out of Egypt. That seems so long ago, and here we are, prisoners again.

Salome: At least we are not slaves, but I'll admit that times are hard enough. I hate those Roman soldiers who are always walking through the market, pinching the fruit, eyeing the maidens. They are an insolent lot.

Mary, mother of James: The men have been gone a long time. I am weary. I think I will go to bed. Tomorrow will be a busy day.

Mary Magdalene: I wish I could relax, but somehow I feel that something is going to happen.

Mary, mother of Mark: What can happen? Only that Peter and the others will return with the Master. After all, this isn't the first time they have gone to the garden.

Mary Magdalene: But it is so late, and today when I was at the market there seemed to be more soldiers than ever. I am worried. I am afraid for the Master.

Salome: I know the high priests hate him, but that is because they have never been able to get the better of him. Do you remember those arguments he had with the scribes? He certainly came out on top.

Mary, mother of James: They don't like to hear him talk about another kingdom. When he cleaned out the temple, that really made the high priests furious.

Salome: Well, it seemed a little tactless. There must have been some other way he could have broken it to the priests that they were not supposed to do that.

Mary, mother of Mark: Nothing would have stopped old Ananias or Caiaphas from selling in the temple except an earthquake. They are always looking for money. For the temple, they say.

Mary Magdalene: That reminds me. Was Judas here tonight? I thought I saw him when I first went in.

Mary, mother of Mark: Yes, he was there, but he seemed different. He acted as if he had something on his mind — something he didn't want to talk about. And once I saw the Master look at him so sadly.

Salome: Judas left early. He didn't go to the garden with the others. Maybe he was trying to figure out a way of getting some more money. He is always asking people to give.

Mary, mother of James: Well, he does handle all the money that comes in.

Salome: It is not his money. He should be more generous. I have to practically hit him when I need money to buy food. If he had his way, we would be out begging.

Mary, mother of Mark: He has grand ideas. He thinks some day he will be the chief administrator for the new kingdom.

Mary Magdalene: *(goes to the edge of the stage)* Listen — do you hear something? It sounds like a lot of shouting.

Mary, mother of James: *(joins her)* Look down there. Do you see lights moving? What is happening? Isn't that where the garden is?

Mary, mother of Mark: I am sure it is nothing serious. Just some people celebrating the Passover not too wisely, nor too well.

Mary Magdalene: I don't like it. I don't remember it happening before on Passover. This is a sacred time.

Mark: *(offstage, banging at the door)* Mother, Mother, let me in! Something has happened.

Mary, mother of Mark: *(goes to door at right rear)* What is it, Mark? You are all out of breath, and look at your tunic! It is torn!

Mark: Mother, they have taken him! He is a prisoner and I don't know what they will do.

Mary, mother of Mark: What do you mean? Who has taken him? And where are all the others?

Mark: We were in the garden, and I am sorry, but we all fell asleep.

Mary Magdalene: Asleep?

Mark: Yes, but the Master woke us, and just then came all the soldiers.

Mary, mother of Mark: Roman soldiers?

Mark: And from the temple, too. They were shouting and yelling and among them was — you won't believe it, and I can't ... *(throws himself in a chair)*

Women: Who? Who? Tell us.

Mark: It was Judas.

Salome: Judas? What was he doing there? Why wasn't he with you?

Mark: He left early and didn't come with us. But there he was with those soldiers, and when he saw the Master he went up to him and ... and ...

Mary, mother of Mark: What did he do? Please, please tell us.

Mark: He kissed him and called him Master.

Salome: What is wrong with that?

Mark: *(jumps up)* Don't you see? That's how they knew the Master. Then the soldiers came up and grabbed him and shouted, "Take him away." We couldn't stop them, although Peter chopped an ear off one of them.

Salome: Good for him.

Mark: But the Master healed him and then went with the soldiers. There he was, walking so calm and so brave, and all around him the men were shouting and calling him names.

Mary Magdalene: Where did the others go? Surely they are with him now.

Mark: I don't know. When I saw him being pulled away I was frightened, so I ran, and when I looked back, all the others were gone, too. I was afraid, so I came here. I must hide. Surely if they have taken the Master, they will take us, too.

Mary, mother of Mark: Relax, my son. Surely they will do nothing tonight. After all, it is still Passover and they cannot call the council at night.

Mark: But it is getting late, and they were dragging him to the high priest's house. I heard one of them say so.

Mary Magdalene: Where was Peter? Was he there?

Mark: The last I saw of him, he was following along, a little ways behind.

(All start to exit. Salome is last.)

Salome: *(turns toward audience)* It is almost dawn. There is nothing we can do tonight. We must wait and pray. Oh, I hope Peter and some of the others are staying with him. He will surely need them now.

(As they exit, the cock crows. A trumpet can be used for this.)

Scene 2

In The Courtyard

Characters
Claudia, wife of Pilate
Julia, Claudia's maid
Pilate

Setting
Open court or stage with a Roman helmet resting on a stand

(Claudia enters, wringing her hands, followed by Julia.)

Claudia: Why am I so restless? What is happening that makes me feel this way? I have been to Jerusalem many times before, but never before has it been like this.

Julia: Perhaps you are not feeling well — perhaps it's the heat.

Claudia: It is because we are in this city. I am always uneasy when we come to Jerusalem, especially during the festivals. The people are so intense, so serious. They never smile or relax and enjoy life as we do in Rome.

Julia: That is because their feasts are different from Roman customs. Especially this one they call Passover.

Claudia: Yes, I know. That is why Pilate makes certain always to be here on this occasion. He is afraid something will happen. He thinks of these people as a superstitious and barbaric lot. And there is always the danger that one of them might rise up to challenge the rule of Rome.

Julia: They would never really dare, my lady. With all the Roman soldiers about, it would not be safe.

Claudia: They do not like us. They hate us. Every time I come here, I vow it will be my last. And yet, if we had not come, I would have never heard about that man, the one they call Jesus. Last night I had the most terrible dreams. I could not sleep. I had a feeling that something dreadful was happening. And in my dreams there was always this man Jesus. Listen — do you hear something? It sounds like shouting. Go and see what it is.

(Julia exits)

Claudia: There is something about this man Jesus. When I first heard him speak, I wasn't impressed. He seemed like an ordinary man. But as I listened, I felt something stir in my heart. I felt at peace. *(paces)*

Julia: *(enters, breathless and in tears)* Oh, my lady, they have arrested the Master. The chief priests have turned him over to the governor. They are asking for his death.

Claudia: How did this happen? Where were his friends? Have they been arrested, too?

Julia: No, only the Master. They arrested him last night in the garden. They had spies who were watching. They didn't dare do anything when he was with the people, but last night he was alone with his friends. They took him to the chief priests, and now they have brought him here.

Claudia: What are they accusing him of? Surely he has done nothing.

Julia: They are jealous of his power over his people. They are afraid and are accusing him of treason.

Claudia: That is impossible. He must not die. He is innocent. Surely my husband can understand that. I have had many dreams about this man Jesus. Go quickly. Tell my husband to have nothing to do with this man. It will go badly for him.

(Julia exits)

Claudia: *(goes to lectern or side of stage — this part may be read)* The whole affair sounds like a nightmare. It cannot be true. There must be some mistake. Only a few days ago, the people were crowding around him to hear his words, and now they have turned. Who are these people? Why would their priests permit such a thing? Surely there are some good men among them.

This is a strange country. Why, oh, why, did we ever come here? There must have been other provinces. But no, it had to be this one. We have been here almost ten years — ten long years away from Rome, my beloved city — the city of beauty, music, feasts, gaiety, and above all, companionship. I grew up in Rome. My father was a wealthy man and a favorite at court. We had a beautiful home with many gardens. My father entertained lavishly. I remember so well those many banquets, the fabulous foods, the fruits, and delicious ice-cold wines — the dancers and the music — the theater and the games. When I married Pilate, I had no idea my life would be spent in a garrison town on a wild coast away from everything. I hate the barren coast of Caesarea and this Jerusalem with its narrow streets, dingy markets, and above all, the people. They are always scowling. They look dirty with their scrawny beards and shabby clothes. Pilate assured me this would not be a long assignment. He is ambitious and believes this is a stepping stone to greater things. It is true that he is in favor at court, but that cannot be said of the people here. They hate us Romans, and I hate them — except — except for one.

I remember the first time I heard of the one they call the Nazarene or Master. My maid, Julia, was late in arriving to dress my hair for a banquet. I scolded her when she ran in breathless. When I asked her where she had been, she told me some strange tale about hearing a man talk near the temple. He spoke of a new world — a new life. I laughed at her. There are many gods in Rome, also many prophets. They are always promising something, but Julia said this man was different. He spoke of a God, an unseen God, who loved his people and said that he had been sent by God to show the way. She told me so many things that I became curious. One day I went with her. He was speaking to a crowd of people near the temple. He did not look very different, but his answers to the questions impressed me. He said there was only one God; that we should love him with all our hearts, and we should also love our neighbors. It sounded so simple. Yet, who is this one God? And how can he be more powerful than all the gods of Rome? And I don't think they have so much power! I do not understand all he is saying, but I know that he is a good man and does not deserve to die.

Julia: *(rushes in)* It is too late. They have persuaded Pilate to give him up. He is to be crucified.

Claudia: *(moves toward Julia)* Did you give my husband my message? Did you tell him about my dreams?

Julia: He paid no attention. He was only listening to the cries of the mob and the priests. Then he washed his hands. I cannot bear it. *(rushes out of room, crying bitterly)*

Claudia: *(again goes to lectern)* All my life I have had dreams. Some of them have been so close to the truth that I have been afraid. I remember the dream I had before we came to this country. I was walking along the shore; the wind was blowing and I was crying. I could not find my husband. Then I saw a boat approaching, and I saw my husband standing in it. Just before it reached the shore, the boat capsized and my husband's body floated onto the sand. I told Pilate of my dream and warned him, but he only laughed. I dreamed again that I was on a high hill and at the bottom were crowds of people yelling and shouting. I stretched out my hands to them, but they kept on yelling. Then my husband stood by my side and suddenly the mob was quiet. But, when I turned to him, he was not there; he was lying dead at the bottom of the hill. For many nights, I have had dreams about this Nazarene. I have seen him standing with my husband who is offering him a platter of gold, but he only shakes his head. Suddenly, the gold turns into wriggling snakes who thrust their fangs into my husband. I dreamed I saw the Master touching a crippled child, and as the child gets up, people grab him, but he disappears. I have seen him looking at me, stretching out his hands, but as I try to walk toward him, my feet seem to sink farther and farther into deep mud. I cannot free myself, and as his hands touch me, I awaken.

(Pilate enters, looking uneasy, and not sure of himself.)

Claudia: *(moves toward Pilate)* What have you done to that man? He is innocent. He has done nothing.

Pilate: Well, he has done enough to turn the chief priests against him, and they are demanding that I do something. As governor, I must listen to their demands.

Claudia: Why do you trust those priests? They are not your friends. They are your enemies.

Pilate: I must keep peace. That is why I am governor. I cannot afford to let one man upset this whole country.

Claudia: They are jealous of him. They have been trying for weeks to catch him. And now they have him. If you listen to them, you are ruined.

Pilate: Well, he ruined the temple offerings when he upset all the tables of the moneychangers and drove them out of the temple. Caiaphas was furious.

Claudia: Didn't you get my messages? Didn't you hear what I said about my dreams?

Pilate: Yes, Julia told me, but they have accused this Jesus of subverting the nation, forbidding payment of tribute to Caesar, and claiming that he is a messiah, a king. That is treason. I'll admit when I first talked to him, I could find no fault nor evidence of such a claim, although he did say his kingdom was not of this world. When I asked him point blank if he was king, he said he was born for this purpose, to bear witness to the truth, whatever that is. Anyhow, I offered to release him, but the priests were furious. They kept yelling he was guilty, and if I released him, I was no friend of Caesar's.

Claudia: They were threatening you, and you listened to them.

Pilate: I listened to the voices of the people who kept yelling for Barabbas, and in accordance with the Passover amnesty, I gave them what they wanted. I thought you said the people loved that man. Well, that crowd out there didn't sound like it.

Claudia: That was the work of the priests stirring up the people. What have you done?

Pilate: There was nothing else to do. When he told about his kingdom, he defied the laws of Rome. There can be no king but Caesar. There was nothing else to do but sentence him to be crucified. But, I'll admit that there *was* something about that man. Even after the flogging by the soldiers, he was able to stand.

Claudia: You had him flogged?

Pilate: That is part of the sentence, but don't blame me. Blame those high priests — the mob. They were the ones that didn't listen. I am here to maintain peace by the authority of Rome. I wash my hands of the whole affair.

Claudia: You cruel, stupid man! This day you have condemned an innocent man, a godly man, to death. You have let your sense of

Roman justice be thwarted by evil men. This act will not be forgotten. I pity you and I pray for you. *(exits)*

Pilate: What else could I do? He admitted he was a king. *(picks up helmet and walks out)*

Scene 3

The Way To Golgotha

Characters
    Mary, mother of Jesus
    Salome, mother of James and John
    Mary, mother of James and Joseph
    Mary, mother of Mark
    John

Setting
    Room in the home of Mary, mother of Jesus

(Mary, mother of Jesus, and Salome are sitting in a small room.)

Mary, mother of Jesus: I am so grateful that you are here with me, Salome. I can hardly believe what you are telling me — that my son has been arrested and is now before the high priest.

Salome: That is why I had to come to you as soon as I could. I was afraid that you would hear it from someone else.

Mary, mother of Jesus: I knew he was celebrating the Passover with his friends and that you and some of the other women were preparing the meal, but please tell me what happened afterward.

Salome: After the meal, they went to the garden. You know how the Master loves that place. It is so peaceful and quiet. As they went down the hill, they were singing. It was a lovely night with a full moon. I cannot bear to think that such beauty could bring forth such evil.

Mary, mother of Jesus: And then?

Salome: We were talking together about the meal, how well everything had gone. Then we heard shouting and yelling, and soon Mark rushed in to tell us that the temple guards had arrested him and were taking him to the high priest.

Mary, mother of Jesus: What happened to the others? Did they arrest them, too?

Salome: No, only the Master. In all the turmoil, Mark said he was afraid and started to run away. He looked back once and saw Peter and John following along, but he didn't see the others.

Mary, mother of Jesus: Why haven't we heard something? It has been hours since they arrested him.

Salome: I am sure there is some mistake. The high priests will have to let him go. After all, he has done nothing.

Mary, mother of Jesus: It is because he speaks the truth and they do not want the truth. They do not understand his mission. They think he has come to destroy the law.

Salome: But the people understand him and love him. Look how they crowd around him, listening to every word, and following him everywhere. Look at the miracles he has done, healing the sick and the blind.

Mary, mother of Jesus: It is for that reason he is more powerful than they are. Where are Peter and John? It is now late morning. They must know something. I must go and find them. I must know what is happening.

Salome: It isn't safe to go out. You must stay here. Surely the high priest will do nothing. After all, it is not lawful to have the Sanhedrin meet at night. They will have to meet in the day, and since it is Passover, I don't think they can do anything.

Mary, mother of Jesus: They hate him. It is because my son speaks the truth. He speaks of the Father's love, and those that follow him will walk not in darkness but in the light. But sometimes I wish he had never left Nazareth, that he had become a carpenter like his father.

Salome: But if he had stayed there, we would never have known him. We would never have known of God's love and his kingdom. Oh, I know we are taught to worship the true God and obey his laws and to take our offerings to the temple, but at times it seems meaningless — just words. But the Master makes it come alive. I am glad he did not stay in Nazareth. What was he like as a boy?

Mary, mother of Jesus: In my heart, he has always been set apart, someone special. I gave thanks to God the night he was born in a stable far from home. He was such a beautiful baby, but I am sure every mother says that. I remember when we went to the temple for the purification. There was a holy man there named Simeon. He blessed my son and said that many would fall and rise because of him. I did not understand, but it was a knife in my heart. After that, we fled to Egypt.

Salome: But you went back to Nazareth later?

Mary, mother of Jesus: It was a good life there. My son was growing up a fine young man and a great comfort to Joseph and me. We used to go to Jerusalem each year for the Passover. I remember one time when he was twelve. When we left with the others to return home, he was not with us. We thought at first he was with another group, but that night he didn't return, so we had to retrace our steps. Three days later, we found him.

Salome: Where was he? You must have been terribly worried.

Mary, mother of Jesus: We were, but there he was in the temple, talking with the rabbis just as naturally as if he had been there all his life. They were asking questions and seemed astonished at his answers.

Salome: You were a good mother, Mary. I am sure you brought him up well in the knowledge and history of our people.

Mary, mother of Jesus: He was a big help when Joseph died. But later, he told me of his mission; that he believed God had sent him to tell people of God's kingdom — that he must go out into the world. Somehow, from that moment, I knew this day would come, but not in this manner.

Salome: Try and be patient. All we know is that he was arrested by the temple guards and brought before the chief priests. Even if they do have a trial, they will need to get witnesses and that takes time.

Mary, mother of Jesus: When men are in power, they can do anything.

(Mary, mother of Mark, and Mary, mother of James, enter.)

Mary, mother of James: Oh, Mary and Salome. It is terrible. The high priests have taken the Master to Pilate. The Sanhedrin has met, and they have said he is guilty of blasphemy. They are telling Pilate that the Master is an enemy of Rome.

Salome: That is utter nonsense. What has he ever done to Rome?

Mary, mother of Mark: They are saying he said he was the Son of God and speaks of his kingdom.

Mary, mother of James: That is enough to get the Romans mad. They can have only one king.

Mary, mother of Jesus: Surely they know he is speaking of the kingdom of God.

Mary, mother of Mark: The high priests are saying he blasphemed; that he is telling lies. They are the ones who are telling lies.

Salome: I cannot understand why the Sanhedrin had him brought before Pilate. They have the right to make decisions in matters like this of blasphemy.

Mary, mother of Mark: It is because they are afraid of what the people will do. If they can bring him before Pilate on a charge of treason, then they will not be guilty of the final decision, and the people cannot turn against them and cause trouble.

Mary, mother of James: Perhaps if he goes before Pilate, he will release him. Pilate doesn't want any trouble. He must know how the people love the Master.

Mary, mother of Mark: He probably doesn't know anything about the people. But, I understand his wife has been seen in the crowds around the Master, and one day she was at the temple when he was speaking. I wonder if she would have any influence?

Mary, mother of James: Do you remember what the Master prophesied? That the temple would be destroyed in three days? That was enough to make Caiaphas furious.

Mary, mother of Jesus: Caiaphas is ruled by his father-in-law, Ananias. I do not trust him at all.

Salome: This must be terrible for you, Mary. How can you bear it?

Mary, mother of Jesus: The hardest part is the waiting and waiting and not knowing. But, I believe in my son. I know he has done nothing wrong. He is only carrying out his mission.

John: *(enters)* Mary, they are giving our Master to Golgotha to be crucified. Pilate has decided. He has given in to the high priests.

All together: Oh, no, no, no.

Mary, mother of Jesus: Oh, my Lord, have mercy on me. *(falls into the arms of John)*

John: Pilate did not want to sentence him. He kept stalling and saying he could find no fault in the Master. But the high priests said the Master was guilty of treason. He had declared himself a king, and Pilate would be responsible to Rome if he did not denounce Jesus. The mob kept yelling at him to free Barabbas and crucify Jesus. It was horrible. I cannot understand how they could turn against him. Just a few days ago, they were waving palms and praising him.

Mary, mother of Mark: It is the work of the priests. They have turned the people against the Master, and they stir up the mobs.

Mary, mother of Jesus: I must go. I must be there.

John: No, Mary, you must not go. It will break your heart to see him. He has been scourged and his back is torn and bleeding. They have placed a crown of thorns on his head which is tearing his skin. It is not safe to go on the streets.

Mary, mother of Jesus: I must go. I must be there to share his agony and suffering. I want to remember in these last hours, those first hours of life when I held him in my arms and the world was before him. Now that world has come to an end. If I could only take away his agony and pain, but I know and I believe that he has come from God and will return to God, and because of him, there will be a new life, a new world, and a new peace. God, give me strength to hold fast. May his love uphold me during these hours to come. Come, let us go.

The Others: We will go with you. *(all slowly leave the stage)*

Scene 4

On The Way To The Tomb

Characters
Mary Magdalene
Salome
Mary, mother of James and Joseph

Setting
Outside Jerusalem

(Mary Magdalene enters, goes to one side if lectern is used or stands in center.)

Mary Magdalene: I am Mary Magdalene. Today is the saddest day of my life. I am on my way to the tomb where lies my Lord and Master. Together with the other women, we will anoint and prepare his body for burial.

So much has happened since the first day he came into my life. I grew up in the town of Magdala, a fishing village on the north side of the Sea of Galilee. It was an important caravan stop — so important, in fact, that a fort was built to protect the trade. My parents were fairly well-to-do, and I had a happy childhood for a short time. At an early age, I began having seizures and spells. Oh, they were not very serious then. I would be playing, when suddenly I would become rigid. I would reel as if I was choking, and I would scream, then fall to the ground. My parents were quite upset, but seemed to believe that as I grew older, the seizures would cease. At first these attacks were infrequent, and there were months at a time between them, but they got worse. I would tear my hair, scratch my face until the blood ran, and foam at the mouth. People said I was possessed by demons. But when the seizures were over, I was all right and would hardly believe that such things were happening.

Then the spells came closer together. Neighbors avoided my parents and children ran from me when they saw me. I never knew when an attack would start, and I was despondent and terrified of what was happening to me. When the spells were upon me, I would lash out at people and mutter and curse in a strange language.

This went on for many years. My parents tried to keep me at home, but I would escape and roam the countryside. Then one day, my parents heard of a rabbi, a man who was going about the countryside with his followers, preaching the kingdom of God. But, the important news to my family was that he was healing people. They took me to the village where he was staying. He was sitting by the lake, and there were people all around him. As my parents dragged me to him, I was seized by demons. Only this time, it was much worse than it had ever been before. My whole body was caught up in some horrible grip that seemed to be squeezing the life out of me. I began screaming and raving, and then I heard a voice say, "Come out of her." I grew more violent — I was being torn in two, and again the voice said, "I command you — come out of her." Suddenly, it was as if a great wind was blowing through my body; I felt it on my hair, my face. I had the sensation of being lifted up, of floating. Then suddenly I was cold and I found myself lying on the ground, crying bitterly.

Then I heard the voice say, "Take her and care for her," and I felt a woman's arms around me. As I looked up, I saw his face. Never will I forget that moment. I was reborn — a new life was surging through me, and as I saw him smiling at me, there was peace within me. The demons were gone, never to return.

I knelt at his feet. How could I ever thank him, this man, this wonderful man, for what he had done? And as I knelt there, two women came to me and washed my face and bound up my hair. I asked them what had happened, and they told me about the rabbi, the Master — this man who was preaching to one and all about the kingdom of God, and that he had come to do the will of the Father. They told me of the crowds of people who came to hear him; of the many he had cured. They told me about his twelve close friends who went with him everywhere, and how they, and some of the other women were with him. The women were there to minister to them, to prepare the food, and to wash and care for them. All they asked was to follow him. I wanted to do this, too. I felt I must follow him where he went.

And I have. I went back to my parents to bid them good-bye, and then I joined the others. I have listened many times as he spoke of God's love; that we were as important to him as each sparrow; that we were to trust in him and to believe.

I saw him heal the sick and restore eyesight to the blind. I watched as he fed the multitude on the hillside, and I shared the bread and fish that were passed among the people. I saw his love for children, his tenderness and care as he held them in his arms, and each day I marveled anew at this Man of God who had come among us.

I heard the scribes and Pharisees as they taunted him and tried to catch him in lies. There were so many that did not understand.

As we were coming to Jerusalem, he told us many things. He said the time was coming when nation would rise against nation, and there would be earthquakes and destruction. Heaven and earth would pass away, but his words would not. He said the Son of Man would be delivered to the chief priests and would be condemned to death. That I could not understand, but he told us to love each other as he had loved us.

Then it happened. The evil forces of men took him and brought him before the high priest, who condemned him and sent him to Pilate, who ordered his crucifixion. And now, he is dead. I cannot believe it. How can I ever forget his agony, his pain, and his anguish as he hung from that horrible cross? The blood dripping from his forehead, the nails piercing his hands.

There was nothing I could do except pray that God would end his suffering. Yet even then, the Master remembered others. I heard him tell the thief beside him on another cross that his sins were forgiven, and he spoke to his mother just before he died. My heart went out to her in her intense suffering. I could not bear it any longer. It grew dark and there were earthquakes and thunderstorms. Then I heard him say, "It is finished." It was over. Those terrible three hours were ended. There was nothing else to do but take down his poor, wounded body.

Joseph of Arimathea had made arrangements to let us use his tomb. He and Nicodemus carried the broken body of our Lord to the tomb, where they sprinkled spices on his body and wrapped him in linen cloths. We followed and saw where they laid him. It was too late to do any more. We would have to return after the Sabbath.

These long hours of waiting and wondering why such a terrible thing had to happen to this man, to this Son of God, I cannot understand. The hours are slowly passing. The night is almost over and it is time to go to the tomb. Salome and Mary, the mother of James and Joseph, are going with me. Together we will anoint his body for burial.

(Salome and Mary, mother of James enter)

Salome: It is so dark I can hardly see the path. Have you been waiting long?

Mary Magdalene: Not very long. Did you have time to get the linen cloths? It being Passover, I know there were no shops open.

Mary, mother of James: Yes, I have had them in a chest for a long time. I had bought them for my own burial. I am glad I had them, but I only wish they were being used for my death instead of the Master's.

Salome: We have gathered all the necessary things. We have the spices; balsam, as well as aloe and myrrh.

Mary Magdalene: I have several vials of ointment and some spikenard. That should be sufficient.

Mary, mother of James: I wonder if we will have trouble pushing the stone away?

Salome: Let's not worry about that until we get there. I only hope there will be no soldiers. They might not let us in the garden.

Mary, mother of James: I don't know why they had to have the soldiers there. Surely they can't expect any trouble at the tomb.

Salome: I agree with you, but we will just have to wait until we get there.

Mary, mother of James: I can hardly bear to think of what we have to do. Only a short time ago he was alive and with us, and now this.

Mary Magdalene: Have you seen any of the others — Peter, John, or Andrew?

Salome: They are staying at a friend's house. They do not believe it is safe to be outside. Anyhow, there is nothing they can do now.

Mary Magdalene: These last few months of following the Master have brought us closer together. I shall never forget his words. I shall keep them in my heart forever.

Salome: The Master was always so kind to us women. He was never angry or impatient with us if the food wasn't always ready or if we were tired.

Mary, mother of James: He was good to many women. Do you remember all the ones he healed, including you, Mary, and Joanna? I especially remember the one who had been ill for over twelve years.

Mary Magdalene: He has been good to all of us. He has made me glad to be a woman and one of his followers. He has given me self-respect, a feeling that I am important to God and that God cares for me. He has given my life new meaning.

Salome: He has done that for all of us. And now we must go. It will soon be dawn, and we must be there early.

Mary, mother of James: This is the last thing we can do for the Master. We will do it together as we have done so many things in the past. And then, what will happen? Where will we go? Who will lead us?

Mary Magdalene: It is in God's hands. We can only do what we have to do. Let us go.

(All exit)

Scene 5

The Waiting Place

Characters
　Mary, sister of Martha
　Martha
　Lazarus

Setting
　Home of Mary, Martha, and Lazarus

(Mary and Martha are preparing the evening meal.)

Mary: My, time goes so fast. Has it been only a week since our Lord was here for supper? It doesn't seem possible.

Martha: It is always such a pleasure when he comes with his friends. I enjoy having them here and preparing the foods I know he likes. I want him to think of our home as his home, too. He is traveling around so much I am sure he doesn't get many decent meals.

Mary: He seems to enjoy yours, Martha, but then you are an excellent cook. I only wish I was half as good as you are. Somehow, I can't seem to really get interested in cooking. Especially when the Master is here.

Martha: I have noticed that, but you manage to do all right. I was surprised, though, when you took that expensive ointment you were saving and used it to anoint his feet when he was here. I thought you were saving that for some special occasion, like, perhaps, your wedding.

Mary: In a way I was. But when I saw him there, I wanted to do something special — something extra — to show how much I loved him and wanted to serve him. I know I can't cook like you do, but I wanted to serve him, too.

Martha: I am sure he appreciated it, and, of course, it was a nice thing to do. He must have been tired after all that walking, and it made the whole place so fragrant. But there was one person who didn't enjoy it.

Mary: You mean Judas?

Martha: He was burning up. He was so angry, he told the Master that it was a crime to waste such expensive ointment. He said that it should have been sold and the money should have been given to the poor.

Mary: Do you remember the Master's answer? He rebuked Judas and told him to leave me alone. Then he said something strange — that I should keep it for the day of his burial; that we always have the poor, but we will not always have him. How could that be, especially since I was already using it?

Martha: Sometimes it is hard to understand what the Master means, but I am glad he told that Judas off. I don't always trust Judas.

Mary: Our Lord must trust him, because he lets him keep the money for them.

Martha: Anyhow, it was a very nice visit. I am glad that Lazarus was here and sitting with him at the table, but I wish the Master could have stayed with us for the Passover.

Mary: Don't you remember? He said we must go to Jerusalem, that the prophecies might be fulfilled. He even talked about going away.

Martha: I am not sure I remember that. I know there was a big crowd outside. There always seems to be people following him.

Mary: That is because they have heard of the good deeds that he has done.

Martha: This time I think they wanted to see Lazarus. They had heard about him and how the Master raised him from the dead. Even now, it is hard for me to believe that Lazarus actually died and is yet alive. There are so many wicked men who hate the Master. Even the priests are jealous of the people who follow him.

Mary: How can they be so blind? Can't they understand that he preaches love and understanding of the Father?

Martha: We can never thank him enough for what he has done for us. Not only has he given us a new understanding of the Father, but he has brought back Lazarus.

Mary: I shall never forget that day. All those people crowding around, waiting to see what would happen.

Martha: Some of them were just curious. And it was dangerous for the Master to be here. He could have been stoned. The Pharisees were just waiting for the opportunity to run and tell what he had done. His disciples knew this, but they came with him.

Mary: He wept when he saw the tomb.

Martha: That is because he loves Lazarus. Now Lazarus is alive and with us.

Mary: Lazarus has changed. He seems to want to be alone and he often goes to the hills.

Martha: Yes, he is different. He is much quieter, and have you noticed? He is much more peaceful. Before, he was always getting into arguments with people, trying to tell them they were wrong, especially about the Master.

Mary: It is late, the evening meal is almost ready. It is not like Lazarus to stay away so long. Perhaps he feels responsible for the hatred and danger from the priests. I wish the Master had stayed with us.

Martha: There is no guarantee that he would have been any safer here. We must pray and wait. But where is Lazarus? The meal is getting cold.

Lazarus: *(enters, breathless and shaken)* It has happened. It has finally happened. The high priests have at last succeeded.

Mary and Martha: *(together)* What has happened? Tell us.

Lazarus: They have taken him.

Martha: Who? And how?

Lazarus: It was right after the Passover meal. The temple guards and the Roman soldiers took the Master captive and led him to the high priest.

Mary: How do you know all this?

Lazarus: Cleopas has just returned from Jerusalem. He says there has been a riot; that the people have turned against our Master.

Martha: I can't believe that. Tell us everything from the beginning. How did they take him? Wasn't he with his friends? Didn't they do anything?

Lazarus: How could a few men stand out against the temple guards? Anyhow, according to Cleopas, they had all gone to the garden after the meal, and the Master was with them. He had gone up the hill a little way and was praying.

Mary: What were the others doing?

Lazarus: They fell asleep. After all, it had been a long day. Anyhow, they were awakened by the Master and the coming of the guards. And guess who was among them — one of his supposed friends!

Mary: Who? Surely none of them would have been with the guards. After all, they were his chosen companions. They were faithful.

Lazarus: It was Judas! He was with the guards, and he came up to the Master, kissed him, and hailed him. That is how the guards knew whom to arrest.

Martha: How awful. I cannot believe that Judas would do that, but somehow he was different from the others. He certainly objected to the oil Mary used on our Master's feet.

Mary: Please, please tell us what happened. Where did they take him?

Lazarus: They took him before the high priest, although I understand they went to his father-in-law first. The Master was alone. All the others had fled, although Peter and John followed along and went to the high priest's home. There he was tried in the early morning. I cannot believe this — there were none who witnessed for him. Where were his friends? Why wasn't I there to testify to what he had done for me? No, he was alone.

(Mary quietly sobs)

Lazarus: The priests then sent him to Pilate, who said he couldn't find anything to condemn him for, but the priests insisted; they said he had made himself king. Pilate gave the order for his crucifixion. After he had been flogged, they gave him his cross to carry, and they made him carry it through the streets so all could see him.

Mary and Martha: *(both sobbing)* Oh, my Lord, my Lord, how could they have done this to you?

Lazarus: When they nailed him to the cross — there were two others who were crucified at the same time — the sky became very dark, and there was an earthquake. He died after the third hour.

Mary: Was he alone at the crucifixion? Were there none to share his pain?

Lazarus: His mother and some of the women were there.

Martha: The Lord have mercy on her.

Lazarus: John helped her home at the end.

Mary: What have they done with him?

Lazarus: They received permission to take his body down, and Joseph of Arimathea has taken it to his tomb. That is all I know. They have sealed the tomb so it cannot be disturbed. Since the next day was the Sabbath, they could do nothing more.

Mary: That was yesterday. All this happened on Friday. I cannot yet believe it. There must be some mistake. Perhaps Cleopas didn't get his story straight.

Lazarus: No, he swears it. He had to get away secretly. All the followers have gone into hiding. They are afraid for their lives. It is not safe to admit that you knew him.

Martha: There is something that we have forgotten. Do you remember when we sent for him when you were ill, Lazarus? He did not come until after you were dead. And later, when I met him on the way, I was weeping. I spoke to him, saying that if he had been here, you would not have died. Do you remember what he told me?

Mary and Lazarus: Tell us again.

Martha: He said, "I am the resurrection and the life. Those who believe in me, even though they die, will live, and everyone who lives and believes in me will never die." Then he asked me if I believed this, and I answered, "Yes, Lord, I believe." And I believe that my Lord is alive today, and forevermore; that he is the Christ, the Son of God who came into this world to save it by his love. I believe that because of him, I, too, shall have eternal life.

Mary and Lazarus: Amen.

Production Notes

www.ingramcontent.com/pod-product-compliance
Lightning Source LLC
Chambersburg PA
CBHW071802040426
42446CB00012B/2677